Fanatical Kink Spoken

SpitVerb Entertainment LLC

Spoken

Fanatical Kink Spoken

Fanatical Kink Poetics ISBN: 1-4140-3272-2
Copyright © 2003 by Jamelle Davenport
Originally published by AuthorHouse

CONTENTS

Chapter 1: Life Views

Spoken

Chapter 2: Religion

Chapter 3: Issues

Chapter 4: Racial Anxieties

CHAPTER 1

LifeViews

Essence of Me

You are filled with the very essence of me

Your skin, your blood

Your bone, your brain

Your spirit and your soul

What you are is who I am

Who I am is what you are

Trust and believe in me

Believe and trust in yourself

For there is no room in the lacking

We are like the sun and the moon

The light that brightens the day

To awaken the body and appreciate nature

The melodious halo to soften the night

To rest the body and comfort nature

Nevertheless, we are the same

We have a purpose

We are existence

Spoken

Nature

Nature

I cannot help but think how marvelous the deity

to put forth all this beauty

Once this beauty had no flaws

Although now the flaws are overwhelming

Still, how blue the sky

With its white clouds, like snow piles on a bright

blue lake

Peaceful

The wind swims over the trees

Dance they do, the leaves, changing colors and

falling

The grass is so green then yellow and sometimes

brown

Captivating

The sun is overpowering

The stars diminish in the day and then sparkle so

bright in the night

The moon so lazy

The snow is so white and dainty

Even earth's catastrophic natural processes are

to marvel at

Nature how beautiful

J.L.Davenport

Day of Reckoning

Adam and Eve's stupidity

Eat of the fruit

Food for the mind

The body

The soul

Knowledge

Shall I drown or dig my hole

In all that I know

Will I be reborn?

Molded from a deeper hole

Than that which the Lord bestowed

Spoken

Earth Screams

Back into the water

Into the Earth

The true maternal birth

Back

Back

The Earth screams

Leave her alone she shows

With all her might

Earthquakes

Floods

Hurricanes

Storms and tornadoes

Leave her alone she shows

The heavens cry

It shrieks at our existence

Shame

Shame

We are

As we die people cry

At our paralyzed last sigh within our still

protruded figures

A soul

Does lift with loss of mass

J.L.Davenport

To absorb into hot planets

Into galaxies where there are billions of stars

Our whole lives we are told that our heavy

bodies are full of soul

Earth reminds us that we are waste

Molded and gravitating

A needed substance

That will one day be

Buried in the wood

Wood derived from the skins of the tree

We once stood as children between those trees

Pissed and played hide n' go seek

The flowers and grass

Poked and withered

Will live upon that dead body

Dissecting into every pore

To plant their roots

Roots we once plucked

So shall they

Because we are but breathing waste

That we abuse the very Earth that is our

existence

We hope Earth will open gates into our make

believe stance of spirits and ghost and show us a

Spoken

supernatural being

Except nature will be there at our end

Our forever host, Earth

Motherland

I love you

My continent

My maternal mother

My obedient sister

Molded dust God formed and structured my

very being

Grew my food

Housed and cleansed me

That worships and conditions me into a man

That seduces and rears me into a woman

When I fall

This continent helped me stand

The strength and protection of my father and

fathers

The love and care of my mother and mothers

The same love you shared with me

I love you my continent

More than the blood, that flows beneath my skin

Heaven preserve you

J.L.Davenport

All of Africa

Each country has sprouted from your splendor

And because of your splendor

The world wreaks havoc on your shores

Your children feel the pain of that infliction

And their blood spilled is abhorred

But you stand strong and beautiful

Even more

Throughout all the despoliation

You are still praiseworthy

All of Africa

Heaven preserve you

Spoken

Blue Nile

Lying on the cool rocky surface of the Blue Nile

It caressing the side of my body with sudsy

leftovers of small waves

My eyes squinting from the suns stare

The bitterness of browning onions and bebere

pepper all through the air

Mingling with incense

Roasting coffee and the popping of dry popcorn

The laughter of the kids

Hopping in and out of shallow waters naked

The man with his beautiful voice singing

His voice sounds as sweet as the music that his

fingertips bring forth from the strings

Forever, tranquil memories

J.L.Davenport

Red Sea

The warm silky touch of the Red Sea

Dripping off my toes

Sliding off the tips of my fingers as I make circles

and waves

Round and round I go

This sea of ages

Priceless

Serene

Coming forth from the heat

I breathe in sweet moist air

I lie back against the hard

Warm

Rock

Its pointy surface to scratch and tickle my skin

The boiling air separating a million times over in

front of my eyes

I fall into the seductive trance that the Sea brings

The ancestry of years and years engulf my

thoughts into the present I see history

History; Beautiful dark people walking along the

calm waters of the Red Sea

Washing the dirt from their feet into the blue

green water

Washing their clothes of all its duty and all their
strains
The women releasing into the water their
menstrual pains
That it would hide them of their unbearable
fluids
And bring back their innocent dark beauty
Present; the Red Sea
Not red at all but of a muddy blue green
I am obliged to hold fast all that was and is on
me
For it is the serenity of the Red Sea that
massages my aggressions
Wakens my obsessions with the old and new
Its warmth and tease painting worlds before my
eyes
The Red Sea

J.L.Davenport

America

The proud

The just

The free

The land where she feeds the world and the

wealthy but so many of her people starve

Starving for the understanding of self

Where the signs on billboards of two hands

black and white

Stand tall over walls

However, the streets see all

The nerve to flower the stripes

Of red, blue and white

In all of its might

When centuries scream of stolen races

From faraway places

The pain and anguish that logo many faces

Cultures lost and nobody cares

Communication of this is rare

The country leads a land of mockery

As the rich, get caviar, crab legs, and too much

wine

Petty criminals get lucky serving time

The streets become elated with bastard children

Spoken

Families broken from oppression that still

lingers

Let the truth be heard!

We fight wars that are others

And those others come to America

And prosper

Let it be known!

The land of the free is the land of the doped

The cheated

The land of the tears

The dreams and wasted years

The land where jobs aren't plenty

Little earned income but high taxes

The land of all races

Races that still have no place in this Anglo-Saxon

land

This is Freedom land to serve the man

Understand?

J.L.Davenport

America Again

America the dream the dreamers dream

America the vision

America

For every star

It is ten thousand folds of suffering

Yeah America

Immigrants and illegal aliens

Hold fast to the dream of democratic equality

Of a homeland free for opportunity and wealth

Of broken chains and endless plains

Many cities of lights with definite plight

So much plentitude

Although behind the flag of

Red, white and blue

Hide many schemers that welcome servitude

Who lie and cheat

Hide centuries of pain

Blood stain, rusty chains

Branders and stolen fame

For their millions

For their billions

However, this is our home

It leeched into the aboriginal bloodline, the

aboriginal culture, their territories, and their
serenity
Left them broken, drunk, high and in dialysis
In a state of paralysis
They exist no more
It leeched into the African bloodline, stealing
from us our African cultures and lineage,
creating perfect slaves that even after freedom
cannot find inner serenity or unity
We can't trace who we are
Therefore we are nobody but the White man's
It leeched into the Mexican bloodline, stealing
from them their territories, history and serenity
Crippling their people's dreams and heritage,
their truths and beliefs, who they were and could
have been
Now they just want to be White
A long time passing, for this pseudo-American
dream
Built from our ancestors hands and broken
backs
Those that built early America under servitude
The only comfort being prayer, song and dance
Lost dreams on top of dreams for one dream

J.L.Davenport

Liberty

Nevertheless you the foreigner who voluntarily
immigrate to this land

You want and you get it, my America

Stepping in with open eyes

Big smiles and big hopes

Turning away from your countries and shedding
your national pride

For equality

Enjoy the ride

It has been a long time coming and you think
you have rebirth from a hard life of pain, a hard
life of tears and hunger

Until you feel the thunder

Now you are looking on the other side

A future foreseen for you and me

You'll be doing more wishing and more
dreaming

Yes we may be freer than the other man in the
sands, across the ocean or the seas

Nevertheless, we cry just as many tears

Shit, pee, and spit

Make love, kiss and fondle

Have babies, make families and feel the burden

Spoken

all the same

America is one big game

Save the American Dream

What about the dream

The American dream

Unity and family

Uncle Sam I'm tired

I'm tired of you

And frankly

I'm tired of calling you uncle

It's a nightmare

There's no peace of mind in a country that is

lying

All the damn time

Tell us the truth Uncle Sam

That you do not know what to do

To fix this country and save our economy

Tell us the truth Uncle Sam

That you're blinded by your own greed

While the economy bleeds empty

What about the dream

The American dream

Unity and family

J.L.Davenport

The American dream is choice

Free speech

Free press

Rights as a human being under the law

However, Uncle Sam's too busy passing bills that amend undermine and are insulting to the rights and health of women in this country

Women who rear children as single parents

And provide as head of household

Women who serve and protect in a land that is attempting to take away one less freedom afforded to them under the law

If the woman is paying health insurance then she has paid her dues to do whatever she wants with her body

But Uncle Sam feels it is his obligation to make the decisions for the FREE women of America

As a woman I am not happy about this

Uncle Sam I am not happy about this

This I am not happy about as a woman

Uncle Sam isn't using his powers to pass a workable job bill proposed by the President

A bill that pays for itself

Creating 2.6 million jobs

Spoken

A bill that will work for the citizens of this

country

It's been FILIBUSTERED

Once again

By Uncle Sam

What about the dream

The American dream

Unity and family

And all of this is happening while,

Over 9% of American citizens are unemployed

That's over 14 million Americans, Uncle Sam

Uncle Sam over 14 million Americans are

unemployed

48 million people in America suffer from food

insecurity, Uncle Sam

Uncle Sam 48 million Americans don't have a

full course meal in their stomachs today

That is double since the year of 2000

Uncle Sam

Hard working Americans

College graduates

Skilled veterans

Trade-smiths

We DON'T NEED YOUR

J.L.Davenport

Token legislation

Token leadership

Political grandstanding

The senate majority- Republicans

And they still can't pass a bill

They can't even explain why they won't pass a
bill

We still got:

Millions of foreclosures and bankruptcies

Shutting down thriving communities

The bills being approved by Uncle Sam aren't

even an infusion into the American job market

Citizens are still unemployed

$434 billion dollars in unemployment paid

Economically we are dying Uncle Sam

Tax payers pay America's debts

Uncle Sam

With lack of jobs

America's bills don't get paid

Small businesses are the engines that keep

America afloat

But all the Republicans are doing is gloat and

play the blame game

Uncle Sam I'm tired

I'm tired of you

And frankly I'm tired of calling you uncle

It's a nightmare

There's no peace of mind in a country that is

lying all the damn time

Tell us the truth Uncle Sam

That you don't know what to do

Blinded by your own greed

While the economy bleeds on empty

What about the dream

The American dream

Unity and family

Red blood in blue rivers

White has dealt their hand

It's been a long time coming

But their children are dying now because papa

can't feed them

Mothers are picking up the gun and delivering

bullets to the temples of their young

Because pride won't let them feed their children

ramen noodles

For too long they have lived good off the backs of

others

Now they ask those others who've eaten ramen

J.L.Davenport

noodles all their lives

Lived in the worst housing

And never enjoyed the American dream

To stand side by side with them

To beseech Uncle Sam

Isn't that grand?

Uncle Sam is a liar

Uncle Sam is a betrayer

We the poor have always known it

And now you know that

Uncle Sam is a liar

Uncle Sam is a betrayer

And frankly I'm tired of calling him uncle

Spoken

Letter of Concern to Africa

The pain of birth

Oh does it hurt

It hurts my womb

It hurts my heart and soul

When birth becomes a curse

O sweet mouth of Africa

Open up and scream

Scream Africa

Scream your pain with rain

Scream for strong crops

And a lot of money

O large eyes of Africa open up and see

Your children suffer and their children suffer

Your children bleed

O strong arms of Africa grab hold of your

continent

Why must you give up, Africa?

Flourish old mother and be kind

O legs of steel and gold stomp into the lands

Your diamond fingers scratch and bleed out the

filth rebirth your lands clean

O generous mother, why are you naive

Do you not see the curse?

J.L.Davenport

Do you not feel the pain and anguish of your
children?
Of your fighters
Of your mothers who bleed and give, birth just
as you once did
Only to lose
One of us is suffering, mother
All of us are suffering, mother
We suffer, you suffer mother
Mother you suffer and we suffer
Look at your people
Look at your countries
Look at your past
Spirits of the slave, be still
Flesh of my flesh be still
Blood of my blood be still
O beautiful, dark, unhappy mother, forgive
Look at your present
Wicked governments and their rebels who
slaughter the innocent and ruin the lands to sand
Greedy, murderers, rapist, plunderers
Rid of them
An eye for an eye
Forgiveness will not suffice this time

Spoken

O Africa

Make it free to call it home

Make us free to look upon it as home

O Africa

How you suffer and we suffer with you

Eve's Spring Pain

I awaken and sing Eve's spring this glorious
morning
A delight of beauty is reborn from cold confines
Heavens soft veil of rain
The suns amber stain, refreshing my beauty
again
I awaken and sing Eve's spring as my petals
bloom of shades that show how delighted and
curious I can be
I awaken and sing Eve's spring even in the
twilight hour
For underneath the stars sultry glare I shine
The mouths of Earth do not criticize me
It desires me
Caresses me
Nourishes me
It loves and perfects me again
I awaken and sing Eve's spring even as the winds
scream blemish after blemish against my beauty
The rain is cold and hard
The suns amber stain is pale and gloomy
Hidden away by the gray of the clouds and the
orange-red imitation of the tree leaves

Spoken

Heaven's soft veil has passed me and hell is eager
to chastise thee
I still sing Eve's spring
As autumn creeps in and quickly disappears
I sing Eve's spring in my last moments
When the sun's handsomeness shines brightly on
another
And the rains that were once soft and fresh are
so far away
The Earth does not caress my withered petals
My beauty is fading, now a soul to compose
alone
In the remnants of Eve's spring
With the residue of something cold and awful
Freezing snow to mask my glow
I sing of pain in quiet confinements once again
Until my beauty is renewed and I am again used
and pursued

J.L.Davenport

Life

To look around this world day to day

To smile

To cry

To fuss

To fight

To live sinful

Godly we try

Then to sleep and die

To wonder about the creator of all things

To wonder why it is that we are even here

Over 5000 years of war and throughout the

drama we still wonder how we will fall

We still marvel at our similarities and our

differences

In the quest to be happy

We ruin all

Although the life that we seek we have

We complicate it beyond belief

The views

All a mystery

Mystery we are

In this creation

A creation that we make more than it is

Spoken

They say life is in the holy book

I am in it

So are you

In this book, you shall see yourself once again

For God created the light of day

Where God's creation- Adam, became all

His woman, Eve, once his prized companion

Are today but sexual prey

Begot from the rib of Adam

But the tree of knowledge distorted her beauty

Like a mirror

She saw herself

And she saw Adam; his nakedness

And evil made night darker than it would ever

be

To suffer, they did

We do still suffer

For we enjoy the life of mystery

Life of fiction

Life of poetry

We live as imitators

Creators

Actors of every word written in the golden book

We live life's desires

J.L.Davenport

Provocative is life
In all its beginning
Never ending
Life's views
We have perfected its story
Mutilated its meaning
Life

The News

The news we see is a constant reminder of the
future
The future so close it is near
Near is now the present
The present now resembles rapture
Let me not awaken and be alone
Let me not be alone when taken into the wings of
love and warmth

PIG

You fools think you rule

Using the law to play God

Wipe the drool from your badges

A badge of honor

A badge of disgrace

You badge wearing skinheads

You bully underprivileged kids

You rape and fabricate

Corrupt and pimp

You trigger happy

Blood thirsty

Steroid taking

Fools

Baton swinging street curser

Stride in your pride

Someone will have your hide

With your belly chafing

Rubbing up against your cheap leather belt

You demon

You punk

Once you were a bullied weakling now you're a

legal thug

You go home to your wife

J.L.Davenport

Eat, fart, and beat her ass
You swear at your kids and make them last
priority
Trying to hide from the reminders of being the
reject you once was
Therefore, you corrupt within the system
Projecting your self-hatred
Onto others
Someone's going to have your hide
Don't mind if I smile
When you die from the stride in your pride
The only ones in line outside the cathedral doors
Will be the racist and whores
Your partners and your wives
Your partner will be banging her that night
Your kids so relieved that they forget to cry
A Satanic following priest thinking about his
1910 gin
And a kid to fondle later
Will send you to your afterlife
Tomorrow a new trainee to take over your seat
To replace your whack offbeat switch on the
street
There is no officer friendly

Spoken

So you get no respect from me
PIG!

Prison Song

He is sitting in his jail cell
Definitely aware that he'll be old as hell
Before he will stare at the beautiful blue sky
Wider than the Lord can provide
That is if he can survive the prison butchers
stolen kitchen knives
The prison guards crooked insight
The sexually frustrated, mind regressed
prisoners fondling their loins in his ass
He is sitting in his jail cell living day after day
Creating colored wigs from his own pubic hair
Cutting a mini skirt from an old pillowcase
He'll have to be somebody's bitch to escape a
deadly fate
Trying to distance his self from the realization of
damnation and find Jesus
It is Heaven that he thinks of...
He is going to hell
He has no fear, no fear at all, but strength
He was born free, yet he is not free

J.L.Davenport

However, until he is free, he will not rest

Although rest will come only in death for he, and

still he will not be free

It is Heaven that he thinks of...

He is going to hell

Thomas A. Dorsey wrote; Take my hand

precious lord...

Yet as this prisoner sings this song of faith and

will, his fingertips are stale from

Rendezvousing with the cement walls in his cell

all night

The warm breeze on his palms is not from fresh

air of the Earth but it is from the swinging girth

of his cellmates yearning

It is Heaven that he thinks of...

He is going to hell

He is not sane

He is talking to the shadows on the cement walls

Becoming familiar with them all

Although there is one that he cannot come to

terms with

He yearns for freedom but his fingerprint burns

a shadow of evil

With a strain and sigh he awakens every

morning, wondering is this the day he will die

With a strain and a sigh he falls to his sleep

wondering is this the night he will die

To be buried in the freedom for sale lot in the

prison plot

Ghetto

I do not know the ghetto

Not personally

I only know the ghettos by what I see displayed

On the television

In the movies

The neighborhoods devouring its children deep

into the potholes that damage their streets

Deep into the waste

I do not know the streets

The ghetto's dead but very alive streets

Some say it is the hood

I do not know the promiscuity

The violence

The misfortune

The weaved out females that stand alone with

their misfortune

Pride exuding from their posterior; they sway

J.L.Davenport

those hips to propel their backsides
The white female hookers
Beat up black and blue whores with their
thinning bleached blond hair
That smile displaying their semen drenched
coffee stained teeth
Nevertheless
I am not blind
I can see the children left behind
Born from young girls who are yet women
I see the whores with their dirty thug pimps
I can drive by and see them giving head on the
rug in some lonely losers back seat
However, I do not know the ghetto
Sometimes I wish I did
Sometimes I wish I had
Because right now life for these people is bad
I want to save the children
I want to save them all
Having to come here day to day trying hard to
do the right thing and save these communities
I am so damn naive
I live under the suburban lights
However, I literally fight for my life in my

urbane community

My dark brown skin is a curse to those who look

at me

My womanhood a slab of meat to desperate

Caucasian men who stare at me

The Anglo-Saxon

How sneaky they can be

Oh, do they pry

Wishing me bad luck

And then there is the Asians wannabe

Caucasians, rolling their eyes

Wishing I'd leave

The surprise they are dealt when having to work

alongside of me

They assume all the brown faces that pass by

Because the numbers are getting high

Suburbia blames me

I assisted and arranged like Harriet Tubman, to

set my people free from their broken

communities

Passing by my roses and mowed grass so green

The birds eating hard breads and seeds

My people say that I am a sellout even after all

my help I am the one they despise

J.L.Davenport

The white people pass by with their smiles,
sneakily calling me a nigger to please their
insanity
My people come around and dance on my lawn
with loudness and slang
And the whites they complain
They exaggerate all my gains as if I am a
criminal
No way have I earned all that I have legally
They say
They fight my property until it is destroyed
I do not know the ghetto
Nevertheless, it feels like the ghetto is trying to
take me
And the whites are trying to send me there

Spoken

False Uplifting

A sad woman always believes she is right

An angry woman will want to fight

In the end, it is only confusion

Free to draw tears

To weep

However, to weep, one must feel the energy of

pain, and then the tears will rise from the soul

The pain is imprinted there

It swells until your whole being rises out with a

howl

The howl into a growl or scream

Tired

Of the swollen skin beneath the caved in space of

thinness

Under your closed, soaked eyelids

The cramping in your chest even after rest

The sore throat, dry and barky

No room for sumptuary

To find your rough spot

And relieve yourself

Of the pressure and stress

Nothing left

Not even rest

J.L.Davenport

The best is yet to come for the time is running on

Breakfast

Lunch and dinner is gone

Your tears are caked upon your face

Judgment has left you in a bad place

You still have the rest of the day to let go and put

a false smile on your face

Homeless

Homeless

Yeah I am

Without a home

Without a bed

To lay my head

Without a decent meal

Generously fed

Without sex when I want it

When I need it

Or want to be

The wet shaky lover on my own sheets

Homeless

Yeah I am

That does not mean I have never had a home

I used to roam around my house naked

The wind from the windows brushing against my

skin

I used to sleep the nights away

In my bubble bath

No longer bubbled

I used to eat when I wanted

Filling my stomach

With the television and music

J.L.Davenport

Playing every station

Homeless

Yeah I am

However, it will not last long

Just another test

I am in a place I do not want to be

With rules to test my every nerve

With people who do not deserve

Anything

With used up everything

However, it is just a test

Because I know as long as I smile

Walk every mile

Keep my head up

Homeless I will not be

Nope not me

For long

Still Homeless

Miserable and drained

Scarcity and hurting

No shelter from the rain or snow

So cold

So cold

Friendless and growing old

Like a used up rag that has no use

Sick and thin like a pole

No food but molded bread and vein sprouted

potatoes from donated shelters

Eyes see through me like nails scratching

The giving heart

Yeah right

That is a start

But rare

In despair I no longer care

Just as you don't care

I am here

You do not see me, that bum on the streets

soaking in the rain

Covered up with soiled newspapers in the snow

freezing cold

You do not see me the person standing long

J.L.Davenport

hours with signs

Begging

I am ashamed

Damn straight, I am ashamed

You just think I like begging

When I am dead

There will be twice of me on these lonely streets

Colder than the nights sky

Thinner than a squinted, eye

Hungry

Color of War

What color is war?

War is the enemy

You kill me

I kill you

We kill each other

They are dying!

Do you hear them screaming?

Do you hear them crying?

The faces on the burning dollar bills

The green occupied with white faces

They are screaming and crying beyond the grave

"No man is good enough to govern another man

without his consent."

Did a white man say that so long ago?

Lies

Lies

Sterilized and refined

Plagiarized and exercised

Knowing but not knowing

Not knowing and yet knowing

That it is still a white lie

They are dying!

Do you hear them screaming?

J.L.Davenport

Do you hear them crying?

Everyone poor and tore down around this

Pseudo-American

Followers

Use to be leaders, European

World

Man, woman and child

Falling off the breast of this Earthly life

Their suckling is incomplete

They are passing away hungry and dehydrated

Bloody and annihilated

Living in hell

Only to go to hell

Echoes of their anorexic shadows fading with a

reminder

A life for a life

The West is the devil incarnate, they say

A life for a life

The West use us as prey

A life for a life

One day they pray

Today they scream revenge

Do you hear them screaming?

Do you hear them crying?

Spoken

The noises so deathly

Like a migraine's rapid pulse hard against the

temples

The air so dark with life after passing life

Going up like silent birds

The stench of their passage

Human waste gases remains

Still the fighting

Still the screaming

Still the crying

Still the dying

A child hides under his mother's sagging breast,

weeping

A father will drag his half-dead body across the

swallowing soil

Wondering if he will ever come home in pieces or

come home at all

Through it all

What remains?

The green remains, damn shame

Large or little

Occupied with white faces

Do you hear them screaming?

Do you hear them crying?

J.L.Davenport

The world's children falling off the of the tree of
life
Can you give to charity please?
America will solicit their citizens
America will lure them
Broadcast with their pious crookedness
Feed the children, please
Whose parents we killed
Rebuild nations
We have torn down
Sure and then
Maybe a movie ten years from now
When many are dead
Lives are stolen
Companies are sought
Cultures are bought out
Racial genocide has almost been a complete
success
As much as possible is westernized
For sure, this is the way and the only way
So they say
"No man is good enough to govern another man,
without that man's consent."
Well when this country kills and bombs all that

he has

This country steals from him all that he knows

and what he knows is truth

To assume his life will be a gift

Let the welfare lines get longer

What color is war?

Green

Occupied with white faces

Color of War II

I will ask again

Do you hear them screaming?

Do you hear them crying?

Back here in the sweet land of the free and rich

The homeless, with their homemade billboard

signs on the highways begging for a little change

for beer and nicotine

Then the persons in debt most of their adult lives

Winning the lottery, so easily,

They are still in debt

Cause that money is not tax-free

Still the riches land on the worlds map

People are starving

One hundred billion pounds of food to waste

J.L.Davenport

35 million Americans hungry

Picking up frozen bodies in the winter, homeless

Run away children selling their bodies, homeless

"No man is good enough to govern another man

without that man's consent."

He should have said

Govern your own, and indulge in the fruits of

your labor

Cause America has its eye on the prize, outside

of its own shores

Is this why my tax dollars flourish?

To enter another door without even a minimum

return to me

Their hands are dirty Uncle Sam

Our hands are dirty Uncle Sam

Your hands are definitely dirty Uncle Sam

I am tired of calling you uncle fool, stealing my

tax dollars for this bull

Corrupting my mind for this bull

Unbalancing my time for this bull

We cannot waste time wiping blood

'Cause my hands and feet hurt like the dickens

with all this non rewarding labor you toss at me

We cannot waste time wiping blood, Sam

Spoken

Our eyes are not just to see death

Do you hear them screaming

Our hands are not just to hold weapons

Do you hear them crying

Our feet are not just to run

Do you hear them screaming

Our hearts are not just to feel pain

Do you hear them crying

Crying tears of blood from mountains

Running on torn skinned up feet

Thirsty and hungry fighters in the white sands

Bodies in the sea

Bodies in the clouds

Bodies still clinging to their souls

Souls dragging eerie shadows

A fight for life

They have a meaning

A fight for rights

They pursue a purpose

Revenge

Freedom

A dream

That is theirs

What is ours?

J.L.Davenport

That we remain first and third world continues
to be barely a third

Why can't we share extravagates of being free?

Of living life as you and me

Whom, might I remind you, would be in a lot of
misery without the third worlds company

Diamonds and gold from Africa, close to illegal

Lead and oil from the east, cheap

Computers and cars from the Asian industry

You see the greedy on the green, occupied with
white faces

Will never be pleased

No, see because servitude equals plentitude

Kiss ass and maybe make first class

Not you

Does not matter what you give but only what you
get that is their motto

Be torn down and stay down, you shall not rise,
that is the surprise on the greedy green

They will take and take and you will see no
wrong but when you need a bit back

You will need to beg and then borrow

That is when it's time to take from the greedy
green occupied with white faces

Spoken

Sam broadcast across the world lies

Sam broadcast across the world fear

Same old Sam crap from a used to be corn fed,

hairy back

Sam, go back to the pigs you swine

Overworking this population into debt and then

you send us off to our deaths

Damn shame the young soldiers do not know

why they will kill or why they will die

Just doing the evil deed civil service for his and

her country

His country will enjoy a nice hot dinner while he

fights

Her country will moan, hump, and sweat sexual

enjoyment on fresh smelling linen as she hides in

the desert sands of another man's land

His country will slobber into supportive pillows

and awaken refreshed when he dies

Her and his country will cry on a flag, shoot

barrels of smoke to salute their service and

choke on song

While their human remains of life are only but

that, red, blue and white on cotton creased sheets

I am sure in their fight for life

J.L.Davenport

As they died a painful death, they saw the light
of the stars

All fifty of them sparkling

Sad even that they had to die for me to live free
and also for you

They experience all that pain, bloodshed,
heartache and confusion

Training was rigorous

Kill or be killed

Loyalty

Be like steel dismiss your humanity!

Training neglects to tell them that they are still
human, killing humans

Humans will be killing them

Penurious incentive if they do survive cause the
plan in them living is a goddamn lie

Does our President have a clue?

What color is war?

Green occupied with white faces

I see no Native on the greedy green

I see no Black on the greedy green

I see no Asian on the greedy green

I see no Mexican on the greedy green

The green is just occupied with white faces and

Spoken

the green is in all the white places

*Dedicated to those soldiers who have fought and
are fighting, who are maimed and will be maimed,
who have lost and will lose, their lives for me... I
wish and I pray there was another way. Thank
you.*

*Dedicated to the disadvantaged and the
underprivileged that work all goddamn day and
give most of their money back in high ass taxes,
those who can't afford a nice meal, nice clothes or
good shoes, them that have no medical but pay
into Medicare and parents who wish that on a day
off of work they had enough energy for their
children and for themselves.*

J.L.Davenport

If

If life could be CD's of your favorite, music

Floating around like clouds

Easy to notice and hear and sing along

Passing us by like airy drip drops

If people could go and come as they please

No hatred

No deception

If life could be choosing your mates

Endless dates

No whores

No scams

Anyone of any race

If life could be romantic

Sensual

If life could be the cause for the erotic tastes

If life could be giving birth to babies with wings

Angels from within

Come, angels out

If life could give you stretch marks but take

them away with a man's kiss

His blissful exquisiteness makes you more

beautiful than a princess

That he could

Spoken

Touch your raw tender flesh

Stretched out

Played out from that angel you birthed

All disfiguration disappears

If life gave us families of geniuses

So wealthy money did not exist

So intelligent and free

No emphasis

Not any on intellectual matters

If we could breathe fresh air

Get along with the bears or wildlife just alike

If we could drink water from the sea

Clean, like crystal blue

If I could go on and on and on

Ifs would never end

If life could be this serene

Would I really be happy?

J.L.Davenport

Thanksgiving

Why am I happy?

Why am I grateful?

Why am I thankful?

Why am I blessed?

About now as I smell the simmer of the stews

The brewing of the cabbage and greens

The baking of the pies

The broiling and frying

Of Thanksgiving, feast

Sweet pheromones of succulent meats to delight

my senses

In admiration it sets in my eyes

Only a few birds fly by and sing

The squirrels quietly waiting for a toss or two of

some unneeded food

The willow tree so tranquil its arms dancing in

the breeze

Why am I happy?

Why am I grateful?

Why am I thankful?

Why am I blessed?

About now as I listen to the smooth beats

The jazzy, sassy, loud, fancy, moving and

grooving, saddening, brightening, soulful

elegance of my

People

I can picture our rainbow lifting higher and

higher on this day

I smell the kitchens in the air

I hear our voices everywhere

I see our smiles and our grace

This day of coming together

Being one

Why am I blessed?

Why am I happy?

Why am I grateful?

Why am I thankful?

It would be because I am alive one more year

It would be because I have one more chance to

sing as I always sing when I open my mouth

It would be because I have another chance to

succeed where I have failed

It would be the blessings to bare children, for I

have gave birth and reared

I am blessed

Most of all it would simply be to be

Blessed abundantly for living at all

J.L.Davenport

Petals, Pedals

Petals

If you could grow and blossom my spirits like the
thickest red rose

Pedals

If you could roll your bike as quick as I flow my
homemade lyrics

With just the beat of my tongue tease

Petals

If you could light up my life like the breath of the
sun does yours

The colors of my soul could soar like the artistry
that flows from your vine

Pedals

If you could spin my life with the breeze

Just a spinning and spinning

Quickly

Petals

If you could open to the waste of my life like you
open to the bees

Let me spill forth my nectar on your leaves

Pedals

Petals

I would be free

Spoken

In Death

I am singing in my sleep

Memorizing poetry in my sleep

Exercising and building up a sweat in my sleep

Crying in my sleep

Forever thinking in my sleep

Humping in my sleep

I am ever awake even in my sleep

The moment is all there is

In death, I will sleep a deep complete sleep

Knowledge

You learn from your mistakes

Mistakes can be forever

A blemish is not a flaw

Pain is but a pleasure

Your enemy can be your friend

Most of your friends are your enemies

An empty belly is actually full

That's because it hurts

We are all created equal

In another world

Good, will come to those who wait

You wait and you'll keep waiting

Give offerings to receive blessings

Do not give to receive because takers don't give

Born to die, die to be born

Everyone and everything in this world is born

and dies

Man woman and child

Beast and environment

Continually passing through birth and death

The breath of life, the last breath, the cycle

miraculous and beautiful

The elaborate wonders of it all

The thought on how and when

Is truly grand

Nevertheless even with all of this wealth

The environment

Having beast and man

How could man reverse the plan?

With his ragged and savage insight, his

intelligence is too great

His mind with his hands can damage

Like many paints tossed on sheet and called art,

unappealing

Man can now create breath and take it away

Once the throes of death was without pain,

without guilt, without shame

Once upon a time, I am sure

J.L.Davenport

That in death the clouds would glide you into the
heavens and the sun would not burn but soothe
Now the clouds are gray, the sun is on fire, and
we have storms ahead

Greedy

You hunger and thirst to be fulfilled
You wish to be fulfilled wherein it brings
substantial filling
Why is this sin?
Because, fulfillment comes from within the need
Wishing and wanting is greedy
You will conceive more than you need
Why must your cup overflow? When it could be
shared and all thirst quenched
Why must your belly rumble for the depletion of
another human being?
To look upon their swollen bellies hurting with
hunger
Greediness comes from wanting, why must your
cup overflow only to waste
This is a sin

Erudition

Erudition is the key

I feed my mind more than my body

Knowledge allows me to grow fastidious and elite

in any area I please

I live in more places than one

I am more things than real life can allow me

Anything that touches the heart and reaches the

soul, but utmost frees my mind and enchants

new things in me

Erudition is the key

CHAPTER 2
Religion

Sin

The wet, rich, Earth springs forth around me
Covering my naked body like a dark sheath
Protecting me from the Sun
Everything gliding tenebrously around my body
The lively smells of leaves are ever so sweet
Imprinting inside my nostrils a dewy perfume
Discreet though enchanting
The last thing my senses will remember before I
am engulfed in a realm of selfish dark creatures
Graceful is thy walk; lazy is thy run, Sin
You leap though sly into my presence with
swamp like eyes, dark and murky, digging
deeper into me than your
Mouth can dine my flesh
Sin is leaving within me scars of worldly hunger
The abuse on my life
Is that I might search for my soul
My soul runs from me, as I am too close to you
Sin
I hunger
The anguish hunger for life, Sin
The anguish hunger to be like you but unlike
you, Sin

J.L.Davenport

See how you see deep into me

My blood screams for you, Sin

Screams out the passions that lay dormant

You release the drum like entity that lay buckled

under my angelic hold, Sin

It beats against your fangs, Sin

Your

Griping jaws, Sin

Your

Thumping tongue, Sin

And

You like it

My Lord what can I do?

I am confused on what to choose

Each way I lose

When I reach for your comfort and

understanding

I am deaf to any direction

When I long for Sins vulgarities

That latch tight to my impurities, and trick me

into ease

His voice is loud and clear and it sounds good

It feels good

At least temporarily

Spoken

Sometimes it seems the same, good and evil
Evil and good
Sometimes it feels as if both serve the same
purpose
Confusion and more confusion

"I"

God said, "I!"
Devil said, "I!"
Competition of two conflicting egos

Agnostic

Do I believe?

Is there a higher entity I wish to grab?

Something more beautiful, more intelligent

Engulfed in more peace than anyone

Anything

Floating high above the clouds

Passing us by like airy drip drops

When I call out in anguish

When I sing songs of praise or mourning

It is to a being

Infested in me by the creativity of this lonely

discontent world perhaps

Or the curiosity of a pessimist beating at the

mind

Painfully

Is it my intuition that tells me to look above and

smile or to close my eyes and believe?

After all the

Mockery

Hatred

Carried on daily

The world with no meaning unless we can be

above all

All was created for us not to rule but to love and
cherish
When I sit serene in my secret vision
Hymns flow around my head in notes bouncing
unknown choruses off my throat
Tears of joy not noticeable to me run like the
Black sea down my cheeks
My eyes swell with life only to dehydrate into the
clouds
I become the character in many books
A closer look
I am the beginning
The beginning
I am the beginning
Words come to me in many languages with great
imagination
I see myself as many and all
All hover around my heart
Finding a thick place to harvest immense beauty
Instilling in my soul a rite of passage and
direction
I cherish this entity
What created me is in me
Peace, love and direction

J.L.Davenport

My heart is resting snug with my soul

I believe

In

Me

Church

We are laughing (ha-ha)

We are smiling (smile)

Eyes closed and dreaming

Swaying and thinking (Moving body back and
forth)

Feet thumping on the floor, shoulders popping

Necks knocking

Hands together and clapping (clap)

Reminiscing to this music

It is playing and the drums are beating

They beat and beat

The bass is strong

The rhythm so rhythmic

The sounds uplifting

Energizing

Mesmerizing

Church

Spoken

Church II

What is a church if it is not a home?

A home is warm and welcoming, not judgmental
and conflicting

What is a church if it is only for the Catholics,
the Baptist, the Pentecostal, the Orthodox, the
Jewish, the Muslim, the Hindu, the Protestant?

Those are not places of worship

But religions who rule conduct and your wallet

Religions with views to confuse and use (let us
not hide from the truth)

Reaching as far as the heart, ridiculing the soul
and tearing at the spirit

Dividing is the essence that is perceived on, when
to, where to, what to do, how to receive this
higher glory

Confusion on what to choose, how to abide by,
how to worship, when to worship, which name to
call and how to call it, he, she, it, scientific
theories, how to pray when to pray, fast, rest,
slave, master

Once a positive, now preposterous disaster that
those Religions have construed

Church is a home

J.L.Davenport

Solid, warm and welcoming
Church is a people
Solid, strong, and glorious
Church is warm, welcoming and embracing

My Lord

My Lord
Look what you have done for me
I am like one with thee
My Lord
Your heavenly sounds caressing me
Warmth burns my heart
Tender in its cradle
No light is brighter
Than the one, you have shown me
My Lord
Look what you have done for me
I am like one with thee
I feel so free like the leaves on the trees
I can see your smile stretching across the sky
miles and miles
The shine in your eyes painting the smooth sky
with surprise
My Lord

Spoken

My Lord

My Lord

Praise

I watch them crying praise

Pathetically, whining like dogs to their master

Who gives them no reply and if they can hear,

they do not understand

For this entity says it is not the voice to hear but

the essence of love to embrace

Do they hear?

Do they really feel?

Do they understand?

"Where are you, who are you, what are you?" I

ask these questions in my head and I judge them

with my eyes.

I watch them disgusted

J.L.Davenport

Eve

Who am I you ask?

Sometimes I ask myself the same questions

It seems that I am many, of that I am sure

My memories are sad ones

My lives are of pain and more pain

I am of honor and dishonor

I am a happy woman, sometimes a scorned
woman

I am creature and beast. I am to lay and be laid

Too many years it seems that my body has been
ravaged

For no moment in time have I felt of anything or
anybody except when it was only Adam, our
paradise, and I

Fear of God

Why fear what is to protect and teach us?
Why fear what we are?
We are created with thirsty hearts and loins-
each alike because one speaks to the other-and,
spirits of souls not in our grasp but on hold for a
future yet untold
Nevertheless, God gives us freedom to blossom
and wither, fall and then blossom again
Even if some shall, blossom and thirst and some
shall bloom and starve
Although, most will fall and never blossom again
For it is the confusion of the fear that is
Instead of the love it should be
Why fear, when I would dream to communicate
and embrace physically this entity
I do not hear nor see

J.L.Davenport

CHAPTER 3

Issues

Motherhood

Motherhood is

Grace

Grace I wish

Fate

Fate maybe

A premonition

Less than likely

A decision

Not always

A smile a few times

Proud

A struggle for sure

A dimple in your life

Guaranteed

We can relate at least most of the human race

Of the good and bad

A rape of the heart from the very start

Maybe a bliss that is quickly distinguished

Divorced and split

The crying and anguish

Wingless beings given to us

To devour our time

Entangle our minds

J.L.Davenport

Sabotage our peace

They grow, grow, and never stop growing

Leaving us broke

Stealing our privacy

Respect outgrown

By the eighth grade

In a daze or the worst way

That is motherhood

It should

It would

It is

However, at times it is good

In the silence of the night

When the moon is half-bright

The smiles that embrace the sleeping child's face

Their sleeping eyes and fetal positioned figures

The sweet smell of their childish sweat

The silky glow of their slobber sliding into the
pillow

Ah,

Reminds you of the beauty

You and your mate

One lousy date

One long wait

To the end of a stressful day

The making love that you both made

In the roughness of the sheets

The orgasm you did not meet with his

The sperm he easily seeded into your womb

The egg that flourished in your tomb

Motherhood

The father who is quickly bothered

That by his feet is a sneak

Out the door without a peek

Never to see him again

Emotional strain

Annoying your once innocent beauty

Your ego dismantled

Self-esteem bleached clean

Motherhood

Stretched out

Fatback

Paddy whack

Give a dog a bone

Over weight

Out of shape

You have extra stock in exercise tapes

Motherhood

J.L.Davenport

Although

At times, it is good

When the bubble bath is hot and sensual

The music plays ecstasy

The movie can be heard and seen

Without mommy

This

And

Mommy that

Mommy replacing the first name

All the same

Motherhood

Really misunderstood

A gift of meaning

It should

Of sharing

It would

Of pleasing

It is

Of giving and not receiving

The notion that you have succeeded in a creation

Motherhood

Most times it is good

Spoken

My Love Child

Baby you are my love child

Everything I want to be

Everything I need to be

I hope you will take from me

The good that I possess

You are a part of me

You are my destiny

I look in the mirror and I see your face

Your tears misplaced

With giggles

Your heart is swelling from my negligence

A young mother still in school

And I work too much

However, everything I do is for you

Without my negligence

We have no future

In first grade

You carry your book bag like a suitcase

Ready for a work day

Instead of a school day

They give you so much homework

There is no time to play

Or talk about the day

J.L.Davenport

Homework before everything

Your eyes are closing

Your thoughts are

Same o same

My feet are hurting from working overtime

My mind is bugging

Picking up college classes with our extra dimes

Childcare is costly

Government assistance is bossy

On the weekends, we try to fit activities in

However, I still cannot squeeze it in

We do not go anywhere

We are tired from the weekday

I am sorry baby

I am sorry baby

My little men

My little woman

In a growing world

Giving you dress shoes and high heels

You have no chance to be a kid

Wearing ties at five

Stockings at nine

I love you

You are my future

If this were my world it would be easier

Mothers Pain

She lays there

Face plump and pale

Eyes wide and dry

She lays there

Her breast thick with milk

Leaking out of her in puddles

She lays there

Her stomach stretched

Wide and hanging over her still beautiful thighs

Covering her shrinking, bleeding beat up lily

She lays there thinking about future years

She lays there

With a smile on her face

Her child lying in her arms wide eyed

She lays there

Blessed

Mother's pain is

A Mother's gain

J.L.Davenport

Joys of My Life

The joys of my life

Are the consistent strife

It is the comfort of my body

Pressed lucratively with my burning shadow, the

sunlight mirrors on my automobile window

It is the forever-saddened twin in my mirror

In which I once saw gracefulness within

A little peace if the world would let it show me a

wide grin

The joys of my life are my anger smacked thickly

across my face like pomade

It shines

It is when you look at me you see it and shudder

Even in the smile and the glitter in my eyes

Yet you still wonder

For my eyes are blank, distant in space

My head is high

I shy away

You still wonder

You wonder if I have a friend

The joys of my life is when a Nobody becomes a

somebody in my life

Because in my life

Spoken

There are too many nobody's

Blood; I beg your pardon?

What kind of family am I in?

That I would wish the worst sin

For them all to end

Then maybe tomorrow I would smile a while

And then take it all back

It is concealed for it hides beneath the skin

The wicked thoughts from within

The ache

Blood thicker than water

I beg your pardon?

I wish to disagree

I wish to make a plea

To be free

Waters been good to me

Cleansed my skin way back when

The pimples popped white from my pores

Grew my hair silky thick

Washed my body of shame

The waters cool my fevers

Washes away the phlegm

That bitters my throat

J.L.Davenport

Water ages me graceful

Never scorns my insides

Like the blood that is shared from you to I

From him to bride

From the bride to her hide I am bore

A woman who cares more for her panties

Deep down

She is tossed

From the hurt and the cost

And the years that she has lost

The hugs and the love

She needs the man up above

A man that does not exist except within the

scriptures where he is bound

And in the minds of the weary he is found

Her confusion a tear in her cycle

Her children lie dormant in her cramps

The tan from the rays her eyes made

Darken up our lives

Masquerade around our childhood

A complete merry go round into our adulthood

Blood is thicker than water

Only skin-deep

What kind of family is this?

Spoken

That I would wish and wish

That the stars do not miss

Lightning's strict dance would strike them or me

I love the rain

I have been crying all my life

I love the storms

They have blown me over

A curiosity

What kind of family will I produce, will I lead?

The one the stars forgot to grant me?

I hope so

Blood is thicker than water; only skin-deep

J.L.Davenport

Standard

I do not know if I found him

Or

He found me

We are together now

More than anything, I am enjoying this small

moment

When I can look over him in silence

He is what society calls standard

He is a middle-aged man

With a distant

Separated family of the sorts

Seems I could get no lower

This is way below my standards

He is an average man

He is not a model type

The type I like

He is the starving for attention kind of man

He is a man with an accent

Seems decent enough

Very honest

He is tall

Medium build

More belly than I would wish

He is hairy

His face is accentuated with a dark brown olive

beauty

Blemish free, unlike me

Boyish features

His eyes

His eyes are haunting dark like marbles

Like a deer's eyes

Captivating

Endless, ever so endless

But

Society calls him standard

J.L.Davenport

Brown Man the World Calls Black

He is alone, with no one to consider

He gives the reigns of his grief a tug too many
times

His reigns will never fall they are a barrier most
of all

His eyes pour forth a stream of rage, which flow
down his cheeks to his breast

Breast, which are covered in scars beaten by his
own hands

He is an actor

A rapper

A singer

An athlete

He is a businessman

A well dresser

He is a deadbeat dad

A thug

A menace

His stride is unique

His strength is overcoming

His weakness he blames on others

As well as his failures

His voice asserts a tone so aggressive

Spoken

At times, you would wish to hold onto him

A tone of terror

Rebelling and at times repelling

One must hold a shield

A tone of power

A tone of fatherly love

He knows his language, but he confuses people

from the outside

And they ridicule him

He enjoys the sound of his own voice and is one

with his demeanor

He has too much in his head

His body is his keeper

His protector

His destroyer

His genital he will flaunt to the entire world

He sexualizes himself

He degrades and disparages his own women

Publicly, it is like a game for him to demean

He is the strongest man alive

Yet he is the weakest man on Earth

His manhood is to emulate

He is a man with no manhood

A brown man the world calls Black

J.L.Davenport

Life Is Bare

When life is bare, it is sweet

It is beautiful and honest

It is love

Bare is the softness of the smooth skin

The beauty illuminating from within

The thought

The essentials of tender love

That only we can give to ourselves

Pure as an angel's day

Is what we are

Is what we should be

Then he comes

Hard and rough like the dry bark of a tree

Telling us what beauty is

What kind of beauty he likes

And we believe him

His mind as empty and sly as a donkey

O' how he detains you

With his stinking mouth

Wet and tarter tongue

Lying lizard of the swamp

With prying eyes on you or a few

He comes to make you gullible

Spoken

To make you unstable

Unsure of yourself

Unbearable

And competitive to other beauties

He comes to tighten your skin

With starvation and drugs

To make you greedy and arrogant

To want and wish

Selling yourself for material things

To lose your patience and therefore your

blessings

To cause you discomfort

For your closeness to his bulky frame

He comes and takes away the light and beauty in

your life

The once sweet and soft little girl

Is now hard and lost and full of anger

J.L.Davenport

Beauty

Beauty

Beauty

Oowee! Baby, baby

Look at sista thick

Thick thighs

Hazel eyes

Cheeks high

And that Ass

I can imagine those big luscious hips

Spread wide

Damn!

Look at her sway from side to side

That is my kind of girl

Big breast

Cleavage

In the chest

Thick chocolate woman

Catch that fish

Catch it

Oowee! Baby, baby

She got them full

Lips

(Licking lips) Thicker than thick

Spoken

Those lips to wrap around this dick

With the quickness

Nut all over her juicy lips

Gum it baby

Gum this big

Fat

Dick

I'd skull her ass until I came

That's one Juicy thick bitch

She looks sweeter than sweet potato pie

I want up in that shit! She got that video body

Young

Fine

Hard

Sit her bodacious ass on my lap

Slap

Tap-tap

That ass

Big O booty

Cutie

Dig all up in her fat, deep, hot and wet

Massage and suck her clitoris

Until she squirts and shit

Who is your daddy bitch?

J.L.Davenport

Damn!

Slide my dick between her breasts

That's one Juicy thick bitch

They did not notice her eyes

With a bright future inside

They did not see her smile

White, fresh and clean

They did not see her style

Conservative

Fine

Mean trend

They did not hear her talk

Sophisticated

No Ebonics

They did not see her ride

Expensive

Up to date

All work

No play

They did not

They only saw the beauty in her hips

How they could handle it

Her beauty was in her sway and smooth legs

Her glossy lips and the way her mouth could be

Spoken

dealt with

Her salon hair in their grips

Her beauty was in the word bitch

Characterization of a today woman

Definition of a female dog

They saw their nut on her gut

They saw her ass fucked rough

They saw her tits

Exposed

Shaking

Jiggling

They saw her lips swell

Sucking on their penises

They did not see the college education

They did not see a sister

A daughter or a beautiful mother someday

They did not see a perfect woman

They did not

They did not see, Beauty

Their definition

Of

Beauty equals BITCH

Our breakdown of self-respect

Our breakdown of self-love

J.L.Davenport

Our inventor of self-disrespect

Our inventor of self-hate

Creator of suicidal lust

A sad lesson

A wicked revelation

Of this generation

Beauty

Come here baby, come here

Come here baby

Come here

Come on baby

I said,

Come here

You see that baby

Yeah

You see it getting bigger baby

Come here

Come closer girl

Bring your sweet cheeks

It likes you

Don't be scared

I said,

Get your ass over here

You're going to like the taste of this

Big dick

Just give it a few

Minutes of your attention

You can make up for

Your prostituting momma's pension

She ain't earned

Come here baby

J.L.Davenport

I am gonna be your daddy now

We gonna love each other

Take care of one another

You want to be my friend to the end

Don'tcha?

I know you do

Come here baby

Come here

That's right

A little closer

Closer

Closer

Hmmm, lay your head on my thigh

Go ahead

Get comfortable

Kiss it baby

Kiss it

Do not be scared

(Man laughing)

Do not cry baby

Dry your eyes

Go ahead kiss it

Kiss it girl

Kiss it harder

Spoken

(Little girl whimpers)

Shut up girl

Touch it

Yes

Touch it!

(Little girl runs away)…

(Girl a little older)…

Come here bitch!

I ain't your bitch

Oh, you my bitch and some other things to

I ain't your bitch, fool!

Oh, you gonna be my bitch today

How little and cute you used to be

Your fat chubby cheeks sucking on everyone's

meat

Just like, I told you to

You used to bring in much loot

Taking care of me and my homies

Come here, bitch

I ain't your bitch

You my bitch and some other things to

You gonna do what I say like before 'cause you

owe me

I took care of you

J.L.Davenport

I brought you in when your momma sold you out

Sipping on the pipe lost in the meth

You owe me

Where your daddy at?

Yeah you remember this package

Go ahead lick your lips

This dick is your friend

Give it a kiss

Lend your hand

I can still feel those hot fleshy cheeks

Your throat choke

Your whimpering voice

So sweet

So young

All for me

Come here bitch

I ain't your bitch

I ain't sucking your dick

You had me before

You will not make me your whore

I can walk out that door

I will not come back no more

Oh you not leaving bitch

Your momma has not paid up shit

Spoken

See look at it this way you're the only way I get
paid
You're my sex slave
I will get paid
You are fifteen; it has been a hell of many years
I doubt your momma even cares, or you would
not be here
Today is your lucky day
'Cause I'm gonna take your virginity
And some other things
Come here bitch
Before you get your head split
Yeah do what I taught you
Dedicated to that child sold to the streets for a
small piece of misery
To that made to be ho, whore, slut, and wish to be
queen of the streets
Dedicated to that masculine creature Jack be
reaper want to be pimp
That crack and dust keeper
Dedicated to the lost
You can be saved, found and turned around
There is light at the end of your misery

J.L.Davenport

CHAPTER 4
Racial Anxieties

Racist

It is not that I do not like the color of your skin

Well maybe I do not like the color of your skin

Nevertheless, you wear it

I do not

I mean you all look the same to me

Do the same things

And

Behave the same way

J.L.Davenport

White Power

Damn you

Damn you

Black boy

Black girl

Reparations you scream

With your killing machines

An army in every hood

Guns and drugs lessens your numbers the way it
should

Damn you

Damn you

All you do is complain

Then ask for financial gain

In all your ignorance

Damn you

Damn you

With your brainless slang

Your rappers and gangs

The loud bass

You are the first race

But in last place

As we say, y'all are a pile of human waste

Damn you

Spoken

Damn you

Damn beggars

Bootleggers

Whores

Damn nappy-headed ugly beast

Polluting our schools with all your Ebonics

Asking for a second chance

A free hand

Bastard kids

Damn you

Your people can be happy only if you are cursed,

downtrodden, and kept in chains

Servitude to cotton plentitude is your virtue

How you make us laugh

That love blinds you

You love humanity, but it does not love you back

It does not want you

I want to scream for suicide

I want to kick your asses but I cannot

Damn all of you

For making me scream horrible things to my

white ancestors

I see my people and I feel shame

What have we gained from owning slave chains?

J.L.Davenport

What have we gained from letting y'all go free?

Damn burdens to the White man

Damn you

If I could choose I would not be you or me

Equality

Who says either of us are free

Black Power

Did you say damn me?

No! DAMN you!

Pale boy

Pale girl

With your ringlets and blue eyes

Damn you

Damn you

Lying ass governments

Prostitution covenants

Drug makers and dealers

Race and culture stealers

Damn you

Damn you

Nosey heathens

Profiteers from deceiving

Pedophile fathers of the church hanging crosses

down between your shirts

Breaking families with vulgar deception

Your unholy perceptions

Damn you

Damn you

Incestual beast

Blood money

J.L.Davenport

You are the NIGGERISH population

You give us that name

By far, you are the nigger

Damn you

You make me laugh

You make me scream and cry

You make me want to kick your ass

And

I can

In the open skirts of the ghetto

I cry to my ancestors

That was sold so boldly

Just like me for centuries, Africa and I have felt

the pain

The blood that flowed on its Eden

To supply you pale demons with ethnic seasons

and build your country out of fear

Of the torture of your devilish imagination and

the smoking bullets in your guns

We mistook for hell

You have no excuse

So stop complaining

Damn you

We live on your lack humanity

Spoken

Wicked

Incapable of fair benefits

If I could choose

I would not be you

I would be me with equality

Back in my beautiful Africa from the beginning

Remember

Remember, remember and remember

How can we remember or forget

A past we do not know

However, the world is destined to show us

Remember, remember and remember

I do not

No matter how much you try to remind my

thoughts

Of memories ashore Africa's dark body

I do not remember

Even I do not know

Neither did my ancestors know

Dream, dream, and dream

I do not

At least not, what you would expect of my

dreams

No matter how much you would try to crucify

my mind

With starving and disease

With people unlike me

I am of the lost cultures, the lost tribes

Discontent lives

Those you stole for your greed

Spoken

Permanently erased from Africa's land of many

I am a tourist

Just like you

A brown not so different from the other browns

Many other things I cannot explain

I cannot dream a dream I cannot remember

I cannot remember a dream I have yet to dream

J.L.Davenport

Indignation

Growing up in a world that is of constant
confusion
Watching as my people go from nothing to
noticed, then something to not noticed and back
to nothing again
I know we were somebody but I do not know
when
My generations got more money to spend but
nothing to show
We got style, fly clothes on our backs
Shoes on our feet
Big houses
Nice cars
Riches baby
But it is all a material
My generation does not know who they are or
where they began
I do not think they give a shit
Shit is life as they put it
You live it as you make it
Disrespect, demean, and bleed
You got me
We can blame it on the white man

Spoken

Uncle Sam

We can blame them immigrants

But in the end who is really to blame

We have had too many today's and tomorrow's

Nothing has changed

Not just in this land but overseas

You dig

I am not talking a hundred years ago, twenty

years ago, and not even last year

I am talking about the seconds

Minutes

Hours

I am talking about today

Today that the lord has made

It's supposed to be a good day

I am not speaking of anyone's world but the

brown man's world

Because

I am brown

We're called Black to the world but who cares

about that

We're stacked with a beautiful shade

Proud

Beautiful browns

J.L.Davenport

Dark to light

I am of the first man and woman the Lord made

Always that

My only real reflection

Today is the same shit that happened yesterday,

and the day before that and so on and so on

We live in the past

A past we do not know

We learn some things here and there, but we do

not know

If we knew the past and the ass kicking, ass

raping, ass kissing our ancestors suffered

How they buffered their nails across one another

Bled and cried on one another

Sold their soul to protect and save one another

The mentality is harsh

The reality is harsher

Let us swoosh back to the beginning...

Who is to blame?

The blame can go around

And I'm tired of being lost

I just really want to be found

I want to end this merry go 'round of confusion

I want my people to take responsibility for their

Spoken

wrongs

The wrongs I witness today

The thuggin

The drug dealing

The gangbanging

The slaying

The whoring

I want us to take responsibility for our wrongs

For our failures

Sometimes I wish we could segregate

Keep something to ourselves

Stop giving the world all we have

Today so many of us have made it

We have accomplished so much

Even though the world is against us

However when we've succeeded

We are called the house nigger

What the hell is a house nigger?

This coming from my own people

I must contribute the downfall of my brotha and

sista over there

Over there

Everywhere

To themselves and the other brotha and sista

J.L.Davenport

around them

Then those who oppress us, will copy us

They have tried to dissolution are beauty and
talent

Merely ruin us of what we are by adopting our
ways and tarnishing them into laughter

To say confused and abused and betrayed by the
human race

I am laughing now

Do da de do boo bop da le la

Would you like to go back...?

Home

To Africa

Africa that large, beautiful continent full of
sickness and death

Where the people live day to day in a curse

Where the animals hide and the trees die and the
grass withers away

The rain refuses to come

No rainbows

You hear the mothers cry

Fathers and sons die

Sisters are deprived

Of their womanhood at such an early age

Not just deprived but ill figured

Politically unstable

Would you like to take that journey with me?

Where the people we see

Do not exactly place in our database

Where the people get our last change

Instead of our poor, illiterate, crack-headed,

HIV communities here receive it

The ones who know us only through their

suffering to compare with ours

Come on

Let us take that journey

Home

Where we are not welcomed with open arms or

smiles of love and acceptance

Let us go home where we can sit at a doorstep

and no one will hear our knocks

Let us go home where our ancestors, ancestors

wallop around in tears soaking up the dry dirt

For they don't know their destination nor their

beginning

Where our ancestors have come back in spirit to

be slapped into pain in their after life

Let us go home...

J.L.Davenport

Where not even a syllable we can recognize but
the wiggly smiles on their face
Would you like to go home?
To the place where you think, your last name
resides
You are so lost
What is wrong, did you see a nose like yours?
Maybe some eyes wide and cunning
Maybe it was a woman that caught your libido
when it was at its end
Maybe it was the soft accent coming out of that
man
Maybe it was the dusty streets
Full of incense and the lyrical beat and charm
The soulful dance, the food, the romance
I know
It is hard
Did it ever cross your mind those faces you see
The sad ones
The angry ones
Even the happy ones in Africa
Those same faces are all around you where
you're at now
See our ancestors cry for us, though they blind

Spoken

us with their rivers of sympathy

Oh man I'm laughing and crying now

This is so deep

So deep I can't truly express myself

I am ashamed

I am mortified

By the existence of imbeciles that are to be my

sistas and brothas

Cousins

Uncles

Aunts

I am sick of the bloodline that flows from you to

me and me to you

Do da de do boo bop da le la

I am not ashamed to be called

A nigger by White people

Hurt maybe but not ashamed

See the word nigger is spoken from the niggers

themselves

It does not have my name in its definition

The word nigger is to contribute to their not

having self-respect

To their jealousy

It's their connection to the blood line of Satan

J.L.Davenport

Satan who could not dig the rules by my God

That my friend is why he wallows deep beneath

my feet burning slowly

But

I do hurt

I hurt because I am human

The hurt comes from my heart reaching out to

slap a brotha or sista who looks like me

Whose mother and father looks like, mines

My hurt comes from deep into my feet, which

controls the stutter of energy it feels

When it wishes to kick into the soul of my own

people whom lash at my dignity

Show me no respect

My own people

Nigga this

Nigga that

I do not think so

What happened to the brotha and sistas we used

to be?

I hurt when nigger comes out of the mouths of

Africans

The people who will look down on me when they

come from the worst

Spoken

The people who will burn me with their starving
eyes
Gang up on me with their twirling tongues
Laugh into my face as if we are not one
To be called a nigger by characteristics more
profound than mines
Their skin so dark it is blue
Noses stretched from ear to ear
Their foreheads pushing out their eyes
Belittled by them tall, slender beauties
With milky brown skin
If it wasn't for our beloved Martin Luther King
the strong, handsome bluntness of our Malcolm
X
They'd still be in Africa looking up instead of
down at me
The shame is
That we could treasure their existence
That we could treasure their countries
Their cultures and their views
And wish the best for them
And then they come to North America
They walk upon the dirt that my great
grandparents for centuries

J.L.Davenport

Suffered to build and

Suffered to achieve respect

They voluntarily immigrate

Only to turn up their noses and say they do not

relate to us

They are we more than anyone is

I am laughing because I am pissed now

I am tired of all the nonsense

I am tired of being...

APE MONKEY

DARK SAVAGE NIGGER

BLACK AFRICAN

I am tired of the movies bullshit

People slashed by the whip for some producer to

go home and joke about, the actor is paid, but

the mind is betrayed

Their minds are being raped

I am tired

Do da de do boo bop da le la

We went from strong, beautiful, people in the

most beautiful place on Earth

AFRICA

The chosen place God had his prints on

Eden is there hidden under the caked dirt and

the dead bodies and the old souls of

Yesterday

I want to be free Dammit

I want to be free from the stories that destruct

our minds

And in time has constructed our ignorance

When our thoughts become passionate to

succeed and live

I will smile every time I see my peoples face

I want that kind of proud pain to surge in me

I want people to look at us as God did

As we are precious to the almighty

For no one is like us

We hold the gifts of heaven

But we lost those gifts

When we betrayed one another

Lusting after everything Satan put before us

When we allowed Satan to have control

Of all our secrets

We are the singers at God's gate

The voices that animate the heavens with peace,

joy

Dance

We are the designated authors to complete a

J.L.Davenport

man's journey

We are the strength that has kept Satan occupied

We dance on his toes

For he cannot get between are force and into

heaven

For we were created in God's righteousness

So therefore, we hold the power to be in him

We are dark because the sun loves to rest against

are skin

The stars like to shine us with jewels

We are brown because it is to remind the world

That once the earth was dark and God created

light to see the beauty he had created

This Earth will be dark again

For the dark is everywhere

I am laughing

Because now I am content once again

Let me dance

Get To Know J.L.Davenport

J.L.Davenport is a Minnesota spoken word artist, a talented writer and songwriter. She loves to share her observations and views on life to dare you to open her books, view the detail of her words and seep deep into her thoughts; reality, find yourself in it.

J.L.Davenport